DISNEY LEARNING

DISNEY
CODING ADVENTURES

First Steps for Kid Coders

Allyssa Loya

Lerner Publications ◆ Minneapolis

Table of Contents

What Is Coding?

How do computers know what to do? Do they have brains? No! A person writes lines of code that tell a computer what to do.

Algorithms

An algorithm is a group of instructions that tells your computer how to solve a problem or finish a job. A lot of code put together makes up an algorithm. Think of one step while you're walking as a line of code. To get outside, you might need an algorithm that starts with ten steps. Next, you open the door, and finally, you step outside.

Looping

Sometimes algorithms include the same lines of code many times in a row. Algorithms use loops to repeat these steps. A loop tells a computer how many times to do the same thing.

An algorithm without a loop may look like this: ⬇⬇⬇⬇

The same algorithm with a loop looks like this: 4 (⬇)

Both examples tell the computer to move down four times. The algorithm with a loop is easier to write. It tells the computer to do the action inside the parentheses four times.

Bugs and Errors

Algorithms don't always work. They may have mistakes called bugs. For example, an algorithm to take two steps forward looks like this: ➡️➡️

The same algorithm with a bug looks like this: ➡️⬅️

Instead of two steps forward, the algorithm says to take one step forward and one step backward. The algorithm has bugs and must be fixed, or resolved.

Conditionals

Conditionals are another type of algorithm. They help a computer make decisions based on different conditions.

Imagine a game character running down a trail. The character meets a wall. Conditional code tells the character to jump over the wall. Conditionals can be shown in flowcharts like the one on page 79.

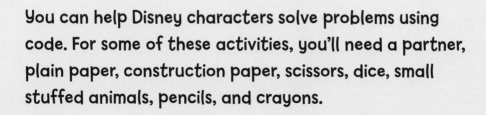

You can help Disney characters solve problems using code. For some of these activities, you'll need a partner, plain paper, construction paper, scissors, dice, small stuffed animals, pencils, and crayons.

ALGORITHMS WITH *FROZEN*

Do You Want to Draw a Snowman?

Anna wants to build a snowman. It's one of her favorite things to do with Elsa. The sisters love working on the snowman together.

What if you wanted to draw the same snowman as a friend did, but you didn't know what steps to take? That's a great way to practice algorithms with a partner! First, grab some paper, pencils, and something to hide your drawing.

Next, draw a snowman. Don't let your partner see it! Then decompose it. That means think about the steps you took to draw it. You'll tell your partner each step to take to draw the same snowman. Be as specific as you can.

When you're done, share your drawings. Are they the same?

When you write an algorithm, you need to be specific so the computer understands your instructions.

Get to Troll Valley!

Anna needs help. Her family needs to get her to Troll Valley as soon as possible!

First, look at the grid on this page. Think about how someone would get from the starting point to Grand Pabbie without hitting anything. Use your finger to count the squares in each direction. Then look at the lines of arrows in the answer choices. Each arrow gives an instruction. Together, the arrows make up a line of code.

Which line of code would get someone from the starting square to Grand Pabbie?

A ↓ ↓ ↓ → → →

B → → ↓ ↓ → ↓

C ↓ → → → ↓ ↓

START			

Try this one next. How would you get from the starting square to Grand Pabbie?

A ➡️⬇️⬇️⬇️➡️➡️

B ➡️➡️➡️⬇️⬇️⬇️

C ⬇️⬇️➡️➡️⬇️⬇️

START

If Anna's parents were in the starting square, how would they get to Grand Pabbie?

A ➡️➡️➡️

B ➡️➡️➡️⬇️⬇️⬇️

C ➡️⬇️⬇️⬇️

Check your answers on page 102.

Saving Anna

Grand Pabbie needs help finding
Anna's memories!

In this activity, you'll write an algorithm to help Grand Pabbie get to Anna's memories. Look at the grid, and decompose the challenge.

On your own paper, draw arrows that will move the wise troll from the starting square to Anna's memories. Watch out for trees and rocks! Think of each arrow as one step of instruction. All the arrows together will make up the algorithm.

Meant-to-Be Handshake

Prince Hans and Anna think they are meant to be together and can finish each other's . . . sandwiches!

Grab a partner, and create a meant-to-be handshake. Each handshake drawing is like one line of code. To make a meant-to-be handshake, you will put the handshake parts together into an algorithm.

First, think through how you want your handshake to look. Use steps from the pictures, or make up your own. Then, on a separate sheet of paper, draw the steps in order. Finally, you and your partner will run, or start, the algorithm and complete the handshake!

Building an Ice Castle

Elsa is on the North Mountain, building the ice castle of her dreams.

If you were building a castle, you might repeat some steps. If you needed to do the same thing many times in your code, you might use a loop. Loops tell computers how many times to do the same thing. That can make writing code go faster.

Both of these algorithms mean to move to the right five times.

$$5 (\Rightarrow) = \Rightarrow\Rightarrow\Rightarrow\Rightarrow\Rightarrow$$

The first one is a loop. It tells us how many times to repeat the same move. Writing the loop is faster than writing out each step.

The main parts of this castle are ready to be put together. Look at the castle pieces, and pick the algorithm that moves each piece to where it should go. Which loop moves wall 1 into place?

A 3(➡)

B 4(⬇)

C 3(⬅)

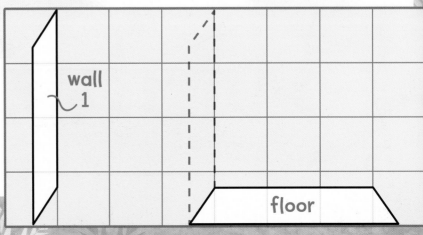

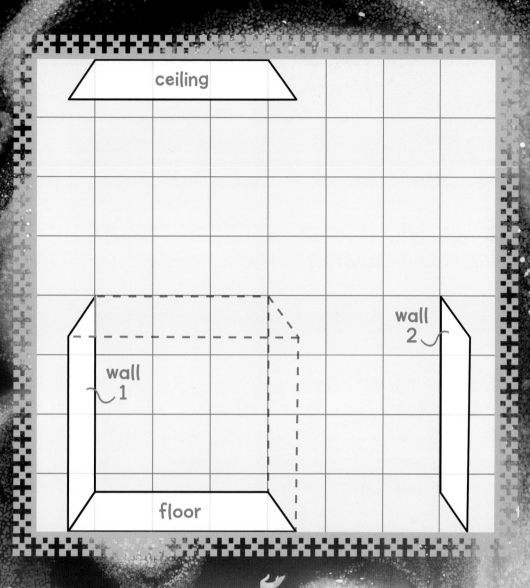

Which loop moves the ceiling into place? Which loop moves wall 2 to where it needs to go?

A 3(➡)

B 4(⬇)

C 3(⬅)

Sven Needs to Eat

Sven is so hungry! He can hardly wait to have a snack.

Look at the grid. You can use loops to create the easiest way for Sven to get to every single carrot. Sven is your starting point. Write loops with arrows, such as 5(➡), on your own paper to create your algorithm.

Escaping the Giant Snowman

Anna, Kristoff, and Olaf are racing away from Elsa's giant snowman. Make them a clear path to follow.

First, draw a grid of at least four rows and four columns on a sheet of paper. Next, add a starting square, an ending square, and trees, rocks, and rivers to some of the squares. Make sure your grid has at least one clear path out.

Then give your grid to a partner. Ask your partner to use arrows and loops to write an algorithm that will get the friends to safety.

Troll Celebration

Kristoff's family of trolls loves to sing and dance.

You and a partner can use algorithms to make up your own dance. When you make up a dance, think about what moves to include. For example, steps might be jump, hands up, touch the floor, and stand up.

Be sure to include all the steps of your dance in order. Use loops if you like! Write the steps down if you need to. Then boogie! When you follow these dance moves, it's as if you are the computer following an algorithm. Have fun!

Let's Go!

Anna's heart is freezing. She needs to get back to Arendelle Castle.

In this project, you will make a path to help Anna get back home. Your partner will write the algorithm. Draw a 6 by 4 grid on a sheet of construction paper. See the grid on the next page for an example. Your grid should fill the whole sheet of paper. Next, cut on the grid's lines to make 24 squares.

Line up your construction paper squares to create a twisty, turning path that will get Anna back home. Look at the example. Use as many squares as you want for your path.

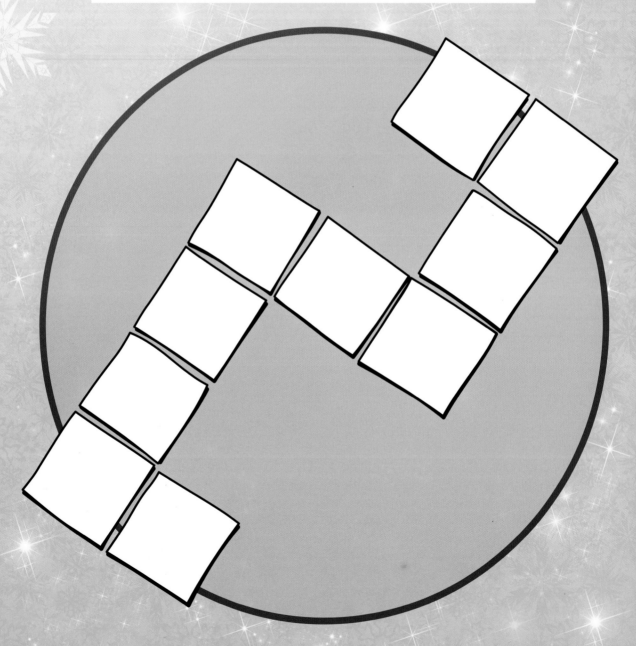

Your partner will decompose the problem. Then, using a clean sheet of paper, your partner will draw arrows to write an algorithm to guide Anna down the mountain. Don't forget about loops!

Run, or begin, the algorithm. If you come across any bugs, or mistakes, in the code, fix them and run the algorithm again.

Make this activity more exciting! Use your squares to make a different path. Add challenges by putting in new squares. Or include trees, logs, or other objects to go around.

In Summer

When it gets hot, Olaf starts to melt. Thankfully, he has Elsa's magic cloud to help him stay frozen. But if that cloud disappears, he'll be a puddle!

Code works great if it's written perfectly. But if there's a bug, a computer can't follow the directions. Look at Olaf's path in the lines of code on the next page. If there's a sun above his path, he needs his cloud. If there is no sun, he can just keep walking. If you don't see a cloud below a sun, that's a bug.

Look through the code to find the bugs. How would you rewrite the lines of code to resolve, or fix, the bugs?

Keep Coding!

Now that you know that algorithms are just sets of clear instructions, you can find lots of chances to practice your coding skills. As you go about your day, think about the steps you are taking. How would you clearly explain them to someone else?

When you make something to eat, do you use a spoon or a fork? Do you need to grab it, then pick it up, and then stir? When you get dressed, which piece of clothing is first? Which arm or leg is first?

When you go ice skating, where do you need to put your feet? Which foot moves first? Do you move forward or backward?

Breaking down tasks in this way helps you think like a coder. What other activities can you write algorithms for?

Have You Seen My Parents?

Dory lost her family. She asks the fish nearby if they've seen her parents. Your partner will pretend to be Dory. Then you can guide Dory to different fish to ask for help.

Cut four squares of paper, and draw fish on them. Put them in different places around the room. Then tell your partner what steps to take to reach each fish. Think of each step as a line of code. Anything your partner will do more than once is a loop. For example, the steps might be: take 3 steps left, take 3 steps forward.

Keep going until your partner
reaches all the fish.

Get to the Jewel of Morro Bay!

Dory remembers where to find her family! She must swim to the Jewel of Morro Bay.

Look at the paths on the next three pages. Then decompose them. That means to think about each step in the path. For each path, choose the looped line of code that will get Dory to her goal.

Swim to the Turtles

Dory needs to catch a ride to find her parents. Choose the answer from the list below that will help her get to the turtle.

A 5(➡️)

B 3(⬆️)

C 5(⬇️)

Check your answers on page 103.

START

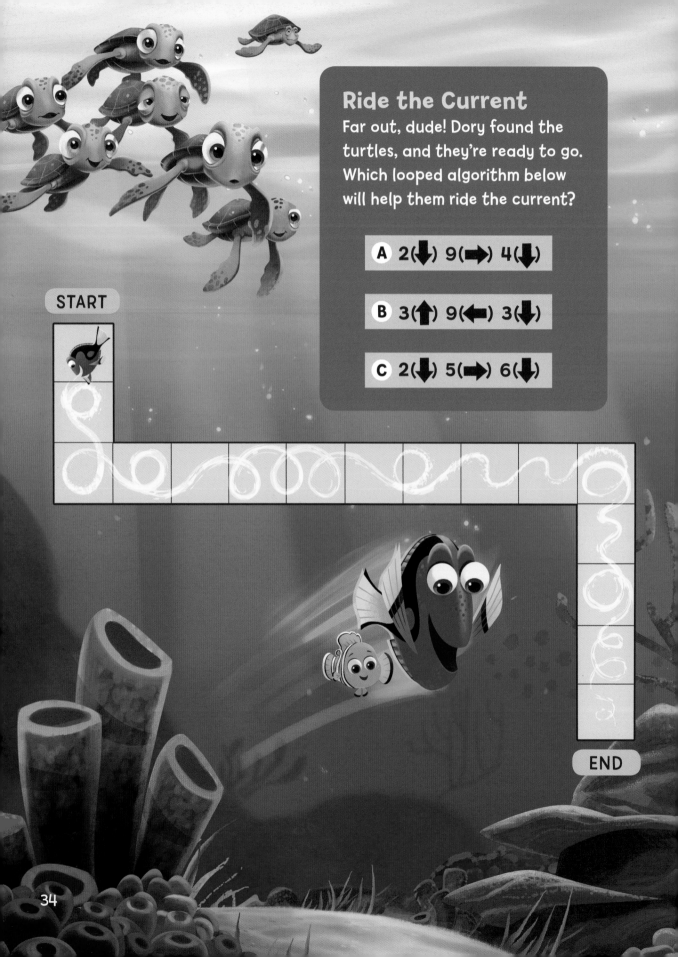

Ride the Current

Far out, dude! Dory found the turtles, and they're ready to go. Which looped algorithm below will help them ride the current?

A   2(⬇) 9(➡) 4(⬇)

B   3(⬆) 9(⬅) 3(⬇)

C   2(⬇) 5(➡) 6(⬇)

START

END

Escape the Squid

Dory is almost there! Choose the looped algorithm from the list below that will help her finish her journey to Morro Bay.

A 4(⬇) 8(⬅) 3(⬆) 6(➡) 2(➡)

B 2(⬇) 8(⬅) 3(⬇) 8(➡) 2(⬇)

C 3(⬅) 3(⬇) 2(⬆) 8(➡) 4(⬇)

START

ESCAPE

35

Keep Gerald off the Rocks

Fluke and Rudder love their rock. They want to keep Gerald off, off, off! They always move toward him and bark when he tries to get on.

Look at the map on page 36. How would you keep Gerald off the rock? Maybe you would move Fluke and Rudder across the rock. Then you could add a line to bark when they reach Gerald. In that case, an algorithm for the map on page 36 might be

3 (➡) Bark!

This algorithm tells Fluke and Rudder to move right three times and then bark at Gerald.

Use looped lines of code to write an algorithm for the map on this page.

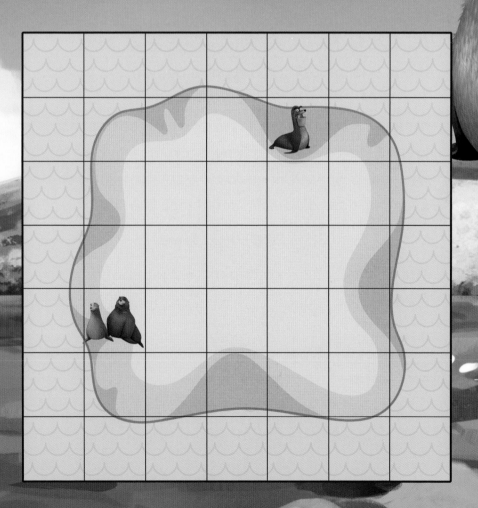

Help Us, Becky! Ooo-Roo!

Nemo and Marlin need help getting to Quarantine. Becky is there to help. Or is she?

Grab a partner and two stuffed toys. The stuffed toys will be Nemo and Marlin. Look around the room, and choose a start point and an end point. The start and end points can be anywhere in the room. On your own paper, write an algorithm with looped lines of code to show Becky how to get to the end. It doesn't have to be a straight line. For example, your algorithm could look like this:

3(⬆) 2(➡) 4(⬆) 2 (➡)

The steps you choose depend on your path through the room.

Your partner will pretend to be Becky and carry the stuffed animals. If your partner follows the algorithm and it doesn't work, that means it has a bug, or mistake. You need to resolve, or fix, it. Rewrite the algorithm until it can run with no bugs. That means your partner can follow the instructions and make it to the end.

Guide Hank to the *Open Ocean* Exhibit

Hank is using a stroller to take Dory to the *Open Ocean* exhibit. He can't see out of the stroller, so Hank has to follow Dory's instructions. Dory should think carefully about each step in the path.

Pretend that you are Dory, giving Hank directions to the *Open Ocean* exhibit. Look at the map on the next page. Then plan each step to guide Hank. Write an algorithm on your own paper that uses loops to get Hank to the exhibit. Watch out for people and objects in your way. When you're done, run your algorithm to see if it works. If there is a bug, resolve it and try again.

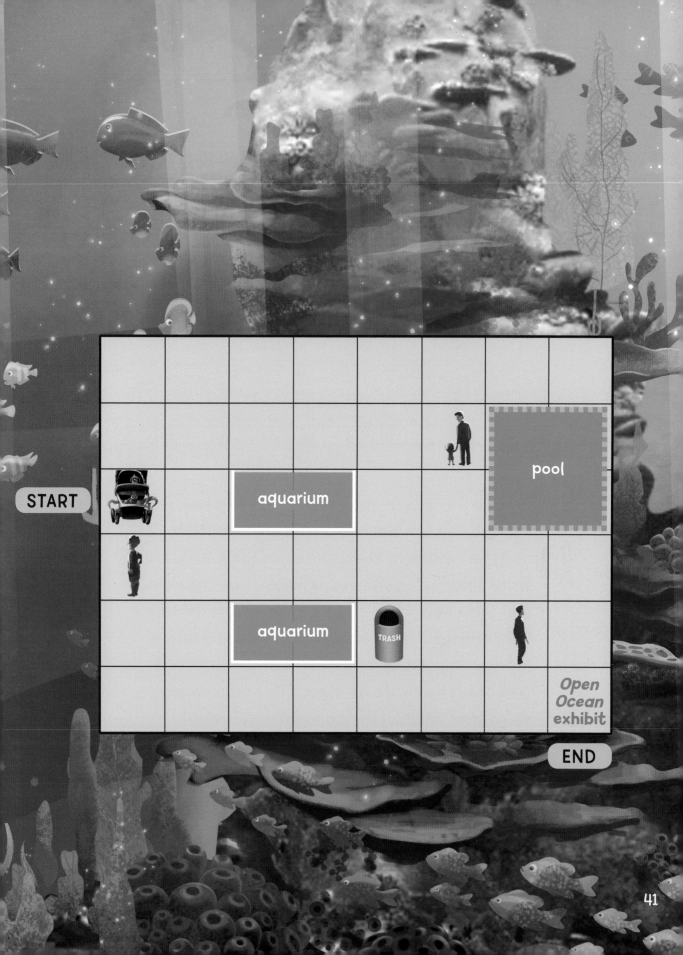

START

aquarium

pool

aquarium

TRASH

Open
Ocean
exhibit

END

The Touch Pool

Oh no! Dory and Hank are trapped in the touch pool! Help them escape.

On your own paper, draw a grid with five rows and five columns like the one on page 43. Put Dory and Hank in one of the squares on the left side. Write "Escape" in one of the squares on the right. Add some hands and rocks to the grid. Make sure Dory and Hank have at least one path to escape.

Show the grid to a partner, and decompose it together. Then write an algorithm using looped steps that will lead Dory and Hank to safety.

Destiny

Destiny wants to help Dory, but the whale shark can't see clearly. Luckily, Bailey the beluga is there to guide Destiny.

You already know how to loop one line of code. Looping doesn't stop there! You can loop multiple lines of code too. For example, say you wanted to move in a square. You could write an algorithm like this: 4(⬆, turn right).

That algorithm tells you to step forward and then turn right. The number says to repeat each step in order four times. You walked in a square!

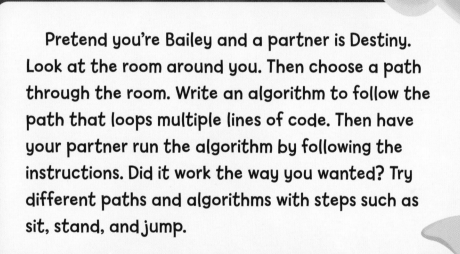

Pretend you're Bailey and a partner is Destiny. Look at the room around you. Then choose a path through the room. Write an algorithm to follow the path that loops multiple lines of code. Then have your partner run the algorithm by following the instructions. Did it work the way you wanted? Try different paths and algorithms with steps such as sit, stand, and jump.

Echolocation

Bailey has a very cool power. His echolocation uses sound to let him sense things he can't even see. Bailey uses this ability to imagine a map of the pipes below the Marine Life Institute.

Look at the pipe on this page. Then write an algorithm to guide Dory through the pipe. Use a loop with multiple lines of code. Run the algorithm when it's finished. Did Dory make it to the end? If not, the algorithm has a bug. Resolve it and try again.

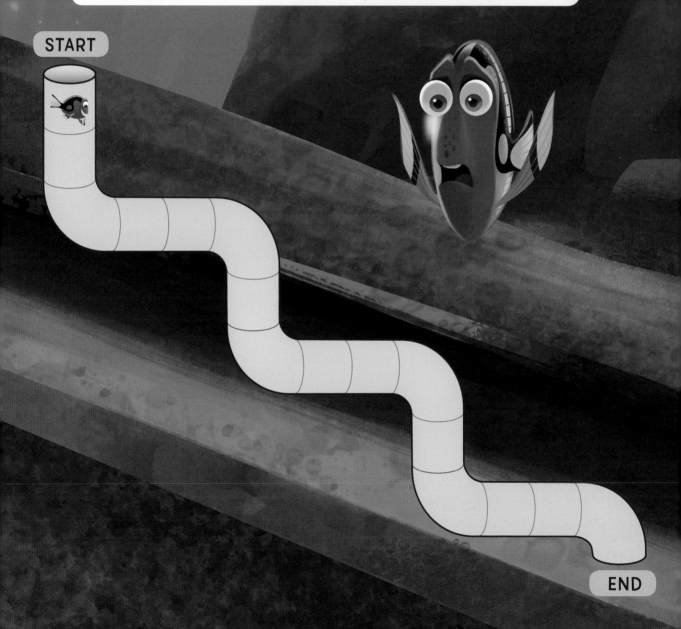

START

END

Escaping the Pipes

Dory is still lost in the pipes. But with Destiny shouting directions, Dory is sure to escape.

When Dory swims to a place where two pipes meet, she must listen for Destiny's directions. Look at the map on the next page. Then look at the lines of code above it. On your own paper, arrange the lines of code into an algorithm that will help Dory escape. Remember, Dory cannot swim through rocks.

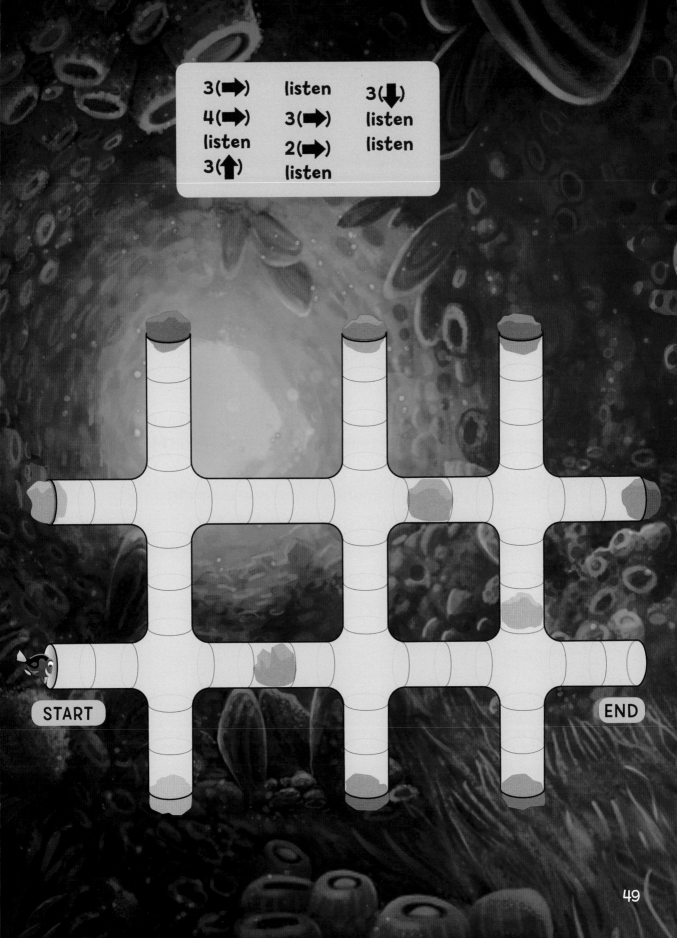

49

Follow the Shells

Make a line of shells that will lead Dory to her family!

In this activity, you will use a do-until loop. A do-until loop keeps going until something happens. Then the loop stops. For example, a do-until loop for Dory might be this: do until you find your parents (swim, search).

Cut a sheet of construction paper into ten pieces. Draw a shell on three of the pieces. Draw Dory's parents on one of the pieces. Then draw rocks on the rest.

Place the rocks on the floor around the room. Put the three shells in a line. Then place Dory's parents at the end of the line.

Ask your partner to be Dory. Your partner will use this do-until loop to search for the shells: do until you find the line of shells (swim, ignore rocks).

Once Dory has found the line of shells, your partner will use this do-until loop to find Dory's parents: do until you find your parents (follow the line of shells, swim).

Keep Coding!

You know that algorithms are just sets of clear instructions. You also know a lot about loops. Think about the steps you repeat during your day.

You repeat steps when you brush your teeth. Tell yourself how many times to loop the brush across your teeth. See if that gets them clean!

When you're walking to the door, guess how many steps it will take to get there. Think about a looped line of code. Then see if you're right.

Look at your food during lunch. How many bites will it take to eat? How many times will you chew each bite?

You can even think about do-until loops during the day. For example,

- do until school is over (listen, learn)
- do until the food is ready to be swallowed (chew)

You can find lots of chances to think about looping!

BUGS AND ERRORS WITH *WRECK-IT RALPH*

Fix It, Felix!

Fix-It Felix fixes everything. He needs to reach the window that Ralph wrecked.

Help Felix reach the broken window and learn about bugs at the same time! Look at the building on the next page. Do you see Felix on the lower-right side? Then look at the list of algorithms below the building. Choose the algorithm that will move Felix to the broken window. If an algorithm doesn't work, it has a bug.

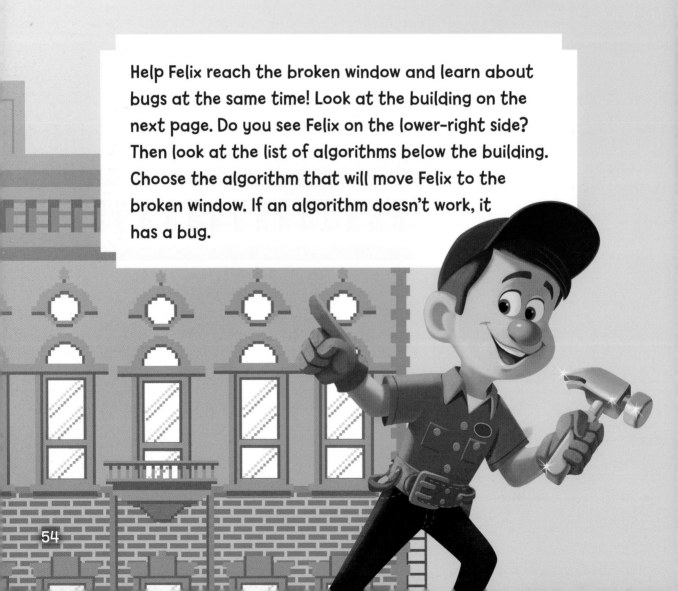

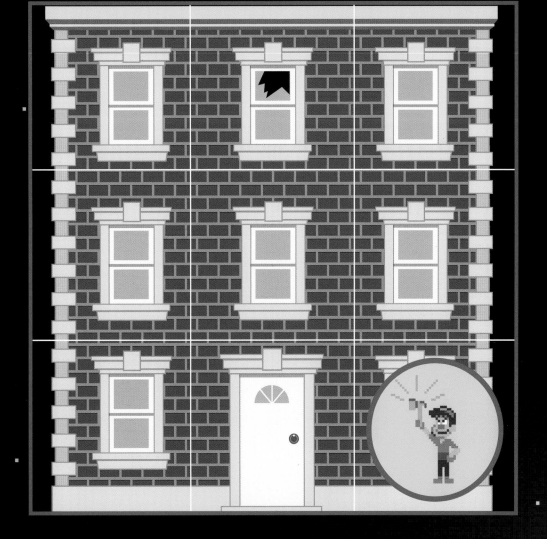

a.

b.

c.

Check your answers on page 104.

Ralph Crashes the Party

The Nicelanders are having a party. Ralph wants something to eat. Help him move across the room to the cake shaped like a building.

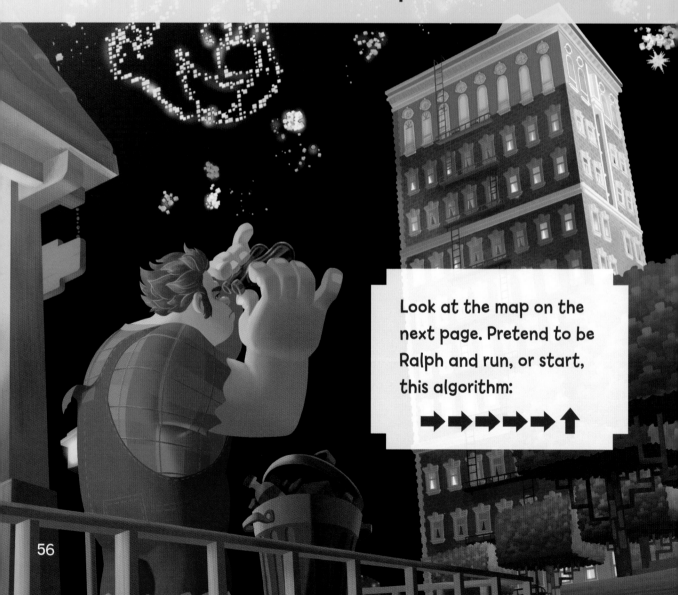

Look at the map on the next page. Pretend to be Ralph and run, or start, this algorithm:

→ → → → → ↑

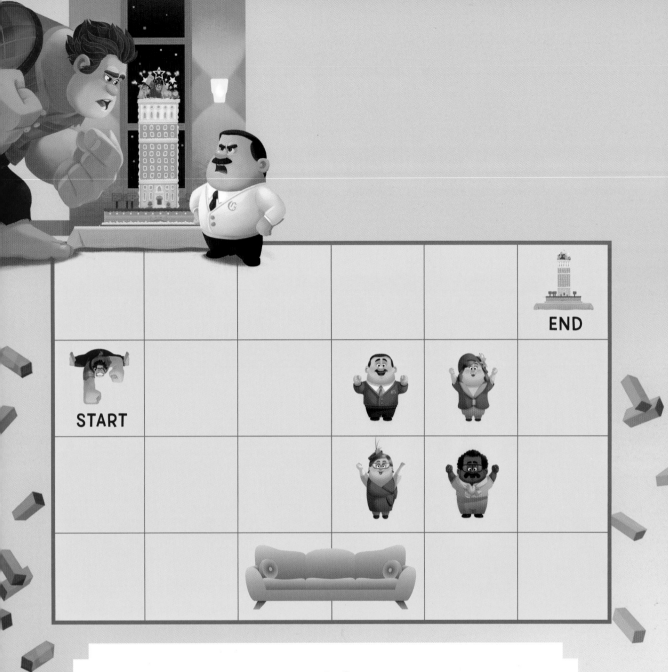

Did you bump into people? If so, the algorithm has bugs. Decompose the problem. That means think about the steps that will get Ralph to the cake. Then write a new algorithm with arrows on your own paper. Avoid bumping into people or the couch. Go to page 104 to see one possible answer.

Hero's Duty

Ralph won the Medal of Heroes! He needs to escape *Hero's Duty* without touching any cybug eggs.

Cut a sheet of construction paper into about twenty egg-shaped pieces. Pretend each piece is a cybug egg. Next, spread the eggs on the floor. Make at least one clear path through the eggs.

Then decompose the problem. On your own paper, write an algorithm to walk across the room without touching any cybug eggs. Use an arrow for each step.

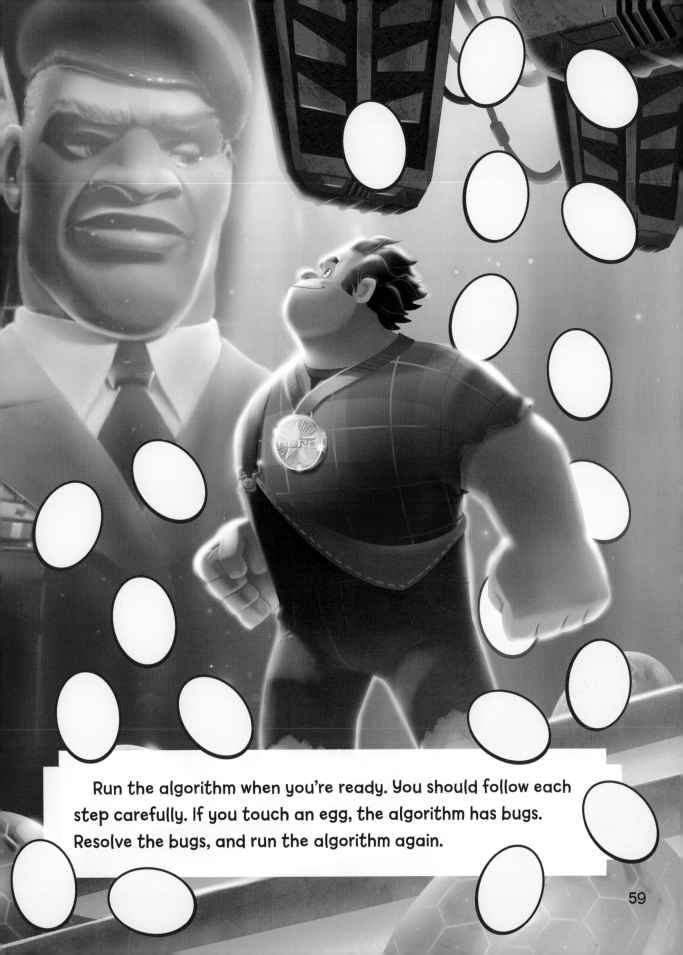

Run the algorithm when you're ready. You should follow each step carefully. If you touch an egg, the algorithm has bugs. Resolve the bugs, and run the algorithm again.

Double Stripe!

The Medal of Heroes is hanging from the top of a candy-cane tree. Ralph wants it back. Can he beat Vanellope to the top of the tree?

Ralph ran this algorithm to reach the medal:

↑ ← ← ← ↑ ↑ ↑ ↑ →

Those steps had bugs. They brought Ralph to a branch with double stripes. Double-striped branches disappear when Ralph touches them. Look at the trees. Think about a path that avoids double stripes. Then write an algorithm on your own paper that brings Ralph to the medal.

END

START

61

Building a Kart

Ralph and Vanellope broke into the kart bakery. Help them build the kart of Vanellope's dreams.

Sometimes code tells a computer to repeat an action. Instead of writing the same instruction many times, you can use loops. Loops tell computers how many times to do the same thing.

Look at the grid on the next page. You could use this algorithm to move Ralph and Vanellope to the gummy worms and then the sprinkles:

Or you could use an algorithm with loops:

The numbers tell a computer how many times to repeat an action. The loops are easier to write.

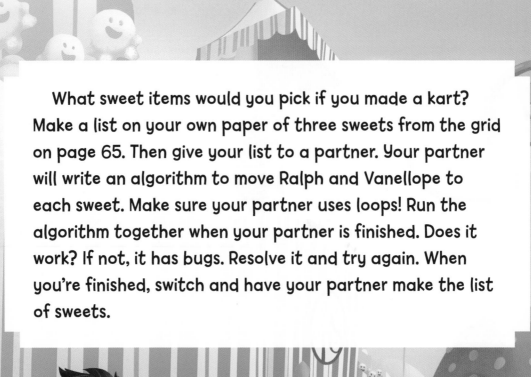

What sweet items would you pick if you made a kart? Make a list on your own paper of three sweets from the grid on page 65. Then give your list to a partner. Your partner will write an algorithm to move Ralph and Vanellope to each sweet. Make sure your partner uses loops! Run the algorithm together when your partner is finished. Does it work? If not, it has bugs. Resolve it and try again. When you're finished, switch and have your partner make the list of sweets.

START

65

Escape the Nesquik-Sand

Felix and Sergeant Calhoun are stuck in Nesquik-sand! If they can make the Laffy Taffy vines laugh, Felix and Calhoun can grab the vines and escape.

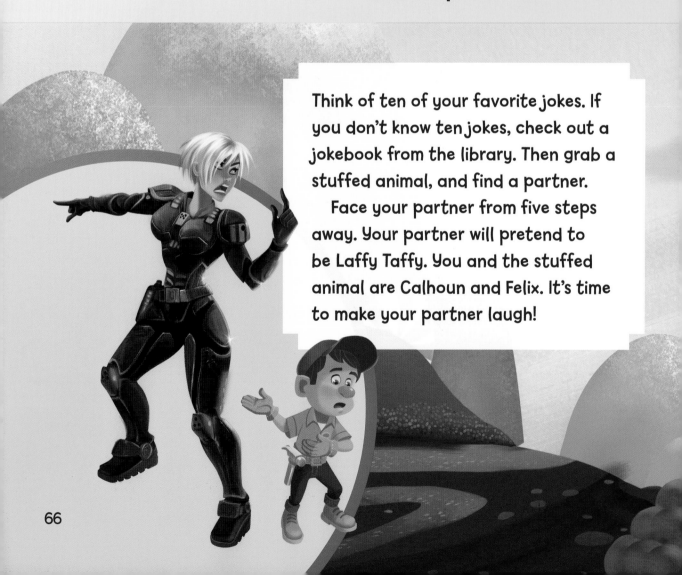

Think of ten of your favorite jokes. If you don't know ten jokes, check out a jokebook from the library. Then grab a stuffed animal, and find a partner.

Face your partner from five steps away. Your partner will pretend to be Laffy Taffy. You and the stuffed animal are Calhoun and Felix. It's time to make your partner laugh!

Think of each joke as a line of code. Read a joke out loud. Did your partner laugh? If so, your partner will take one step forward. If your partner didn't laugh, the joke has a bug. Move on to the next joke. Calhoun and Felix will be saved when Laffy Taffy laughs five times. And you'll have an algorithm of funny jokes with no bugs!

Learning to Drive

Vanellope wants to race. She practices with Ralph inside Diet Cola Mountain.

Look at the paths on the next page. Vanellope can drive straight if the path is clear. But if there's a hole in the path, she must swerve to avoid it. Each hole should have a swerve symbol below it. If it doesn't, it has bugs.

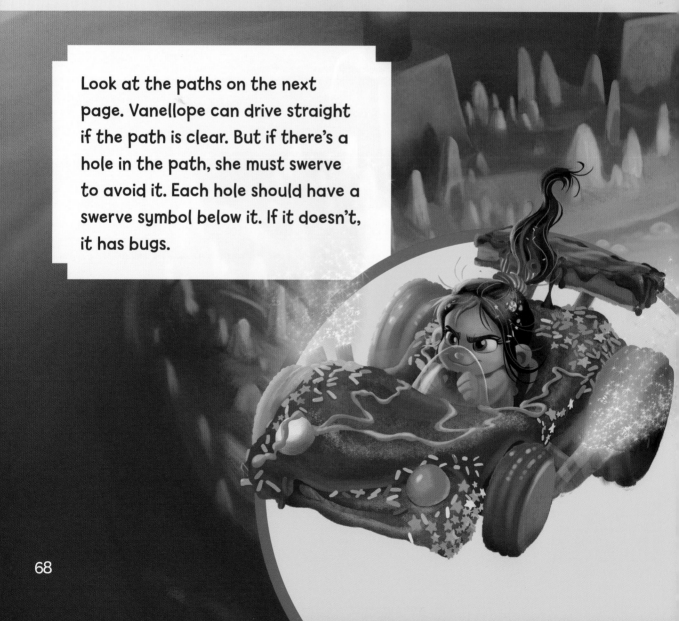

Run the algorithm below each path. Did you find all the bugs? Write new algorithms on your own paper that will get Vanellope to the end of each path.

drive straight = ➡

swerve = 〰➡

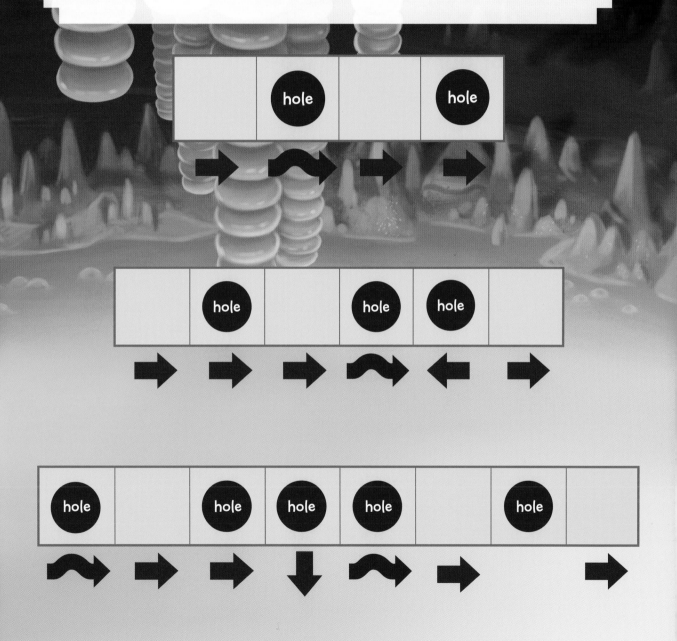

Random Roster Race

It's time for the Random Roster Race. Watch out for gumballs and ice-cream attacks!

Cut about twenty squares from construction paper. Make the squares the same size. Draw Vanellope on one square. Draw a finish line on another square. Set the two squares aside.

Next, draw ice-cream attacks on two blank squares. Put gumball attacks on two different squares. Turn over the four attack squares, and mix them with the blank squares. Lay all the squares facedown in a grid like the one on the next page. Make Vanellope the lower-left square. Put the Finish Line square in the upper right. Vanellope and the Finish Line should be facing up so you can see where they are.

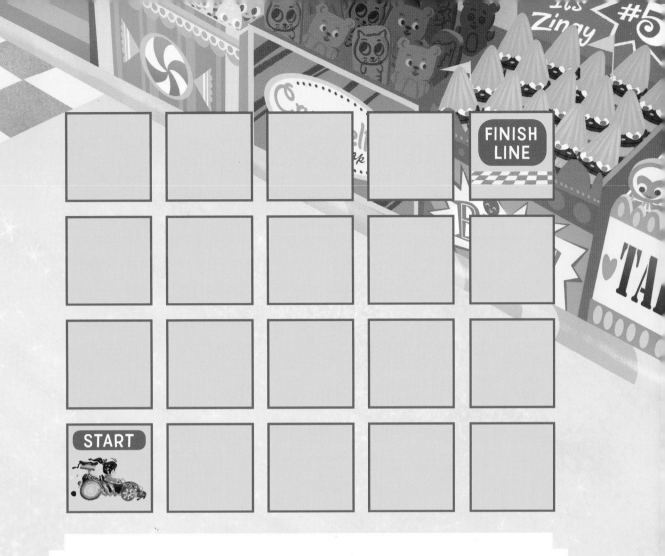

FINISH LINE

START

Write an algorithm on plain paper to get Vanellope to the Finish Line. Remember to use looped lines of code. Run the algorithm, and turn the squares over one by one. If you run into a trap, that means your algorithm has a bug. Rewrite it to go around the bug. Keep going until your algorithm reaches the Finish Line.

Diet Cola Mountain

Ralph's friends are trapped by cybugs! He can save them if he smashes the top of Diet Cola Mountain. But first, he needs to get up there.

Ralph can't climb with all these cybugs in the way. He needs to push away each cybug before he can do the next step. Ralph tried to follow this algorithm to climb the mountain:

2(⬆) 2(➡) 3(⬆) 3(push) 2(⬆) ➡ 2(push)

END

START

The algorithm has bugs, though. The steps are in the wrong order.

Look at the grid on this page. Then fix the algorithm. Change the order of the steps until it brings Ralph to the top of Diet Cola Mountain.

Fixing *Sugar Rush*

The cybugs are gone! But they left behind a big mess. *Sugar Rush* needs to be fixed.

In this project, you and your partner will each draw a grid like the one on the next page. Draw Fix-It Felix in the upper-left square. Add Sour Bill to five of the squares. These are the places where the world of *Sugar Rush* is broken, or has errors. You can put Sour Bill anywhere.

Trade grids with your partner. Write an algorithm to move Fix-It Felix to each square where Sour Bill appears on your partner's grid. Use Felix's hammer to fix each error. For example, this algorithm could fix the grid on page 75:

⬇ 🔨 2(⬇) 🔨 2(➡) 🔨 3(⬆) 🔨 3(➡) 2(⬇) 🔨

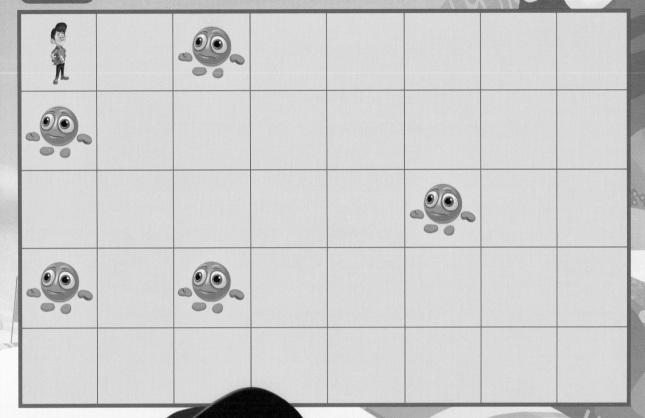

Does your algorithm fix every square where Sour Bill appears on your partner's grid? If not, resolve the bugs in your algorithm and run it again.

Keep Coding!

After learning about bugs and errors, you may start seeing them everywhere. Mistakes people make are like bugs. Think about mistakes you see in your daily life.

Was the school bus late in the morning? Did you trip walking up the steps? Did your pencil break? Did your friend drop some food during lunch?

When a mistake happens, think about algorithms. What steps led to the mistake? Was your shoelace untied? Maybe you pressed too hard on your pencil. Then think about how to fix the error and avoid the mistake in the future. Soon you'll be great at spotting and fixing bugs!

Strike a Super Pose

The Incredibles strike super poses as they keep the city safe.

Find a partner. You'll pretend to be one of the Supers and strike poses. Face your partner from a few steps away. Your partner will count to three and then choose to either show you a thumbs-up or do nothing. Look at the conditional flowchart on the next page. Follow the flowchart's path on the right if your partner does nothing. That path leads to the action "Stand still." But if your partner gives you a thumbs-up, follow the left path. It's time to strike a pose!

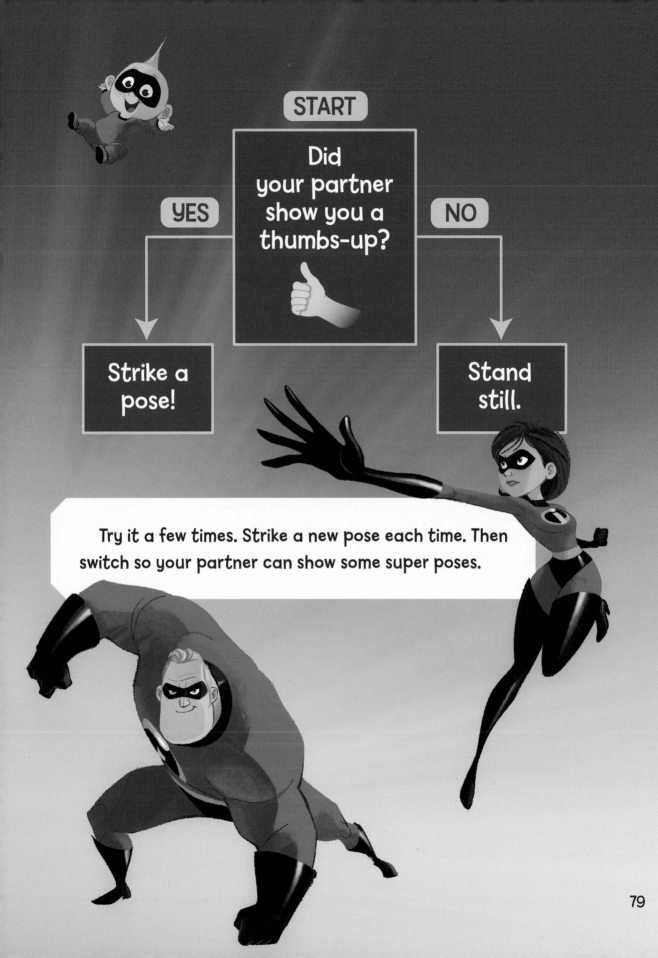

START

Did your partner show you a thumbs-up?

YES

NO

Strike a pose!

Stand still.

Try it a few times. Strike a new pose each time. Then switch so your partner can show some super poses.

Digging under the City

The Underminer is digging under the city to find bank vaults. He wants to steal the money inside them!

If the Underminer is not near a bank vault, he keeps digging. What will he do if he is near a vault? The conditional flowchart on the next page has a blank space. Look at the list of answer choices. On your own paper, write down the choice that the Underminer will take to steal the money from inside the vault.

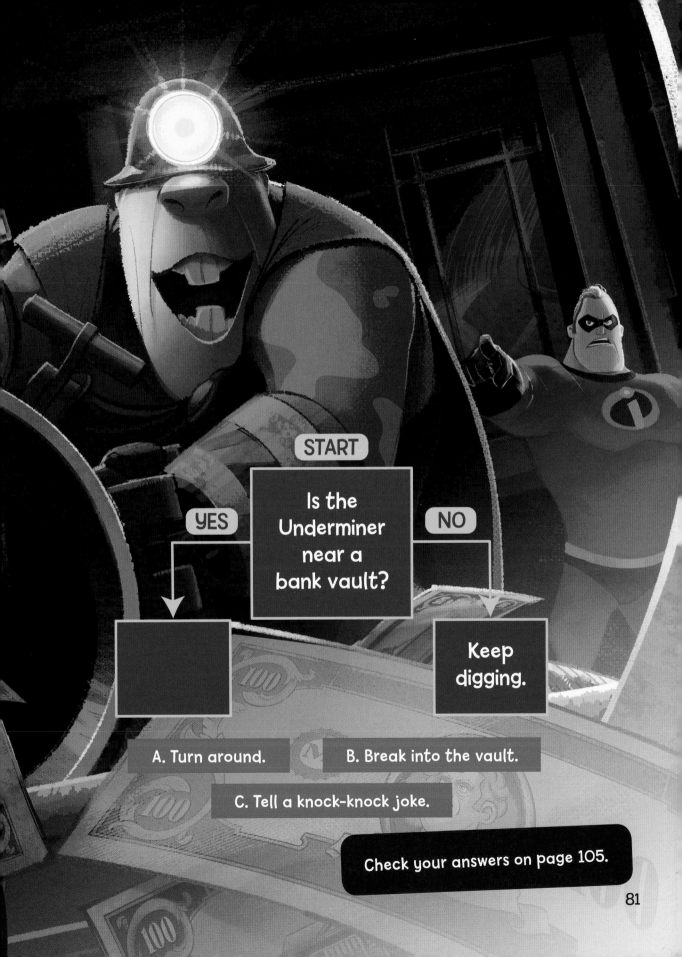

START

Is the Underminer near a bank vault?

YES

NO

Keep digging.

A. Turn around.

B. Break into the vault.

C. Tell a knock-knock joke.

Check your answers on page 105.

An Awesome New House

The Incredibles moved into a new house.
Help Dash explore their home.

Dash keeps bumping into things in the living room. He can run straight if no furniture is in his path. But he needs to turn if furniture blocks the way. Draw a flowchart on your own paper. It should look like the flowchart on page 83. Next, look at the list of actions. Choose one action to fill in each blank square. The flowchart should help Dash move around without bumping into furniture.

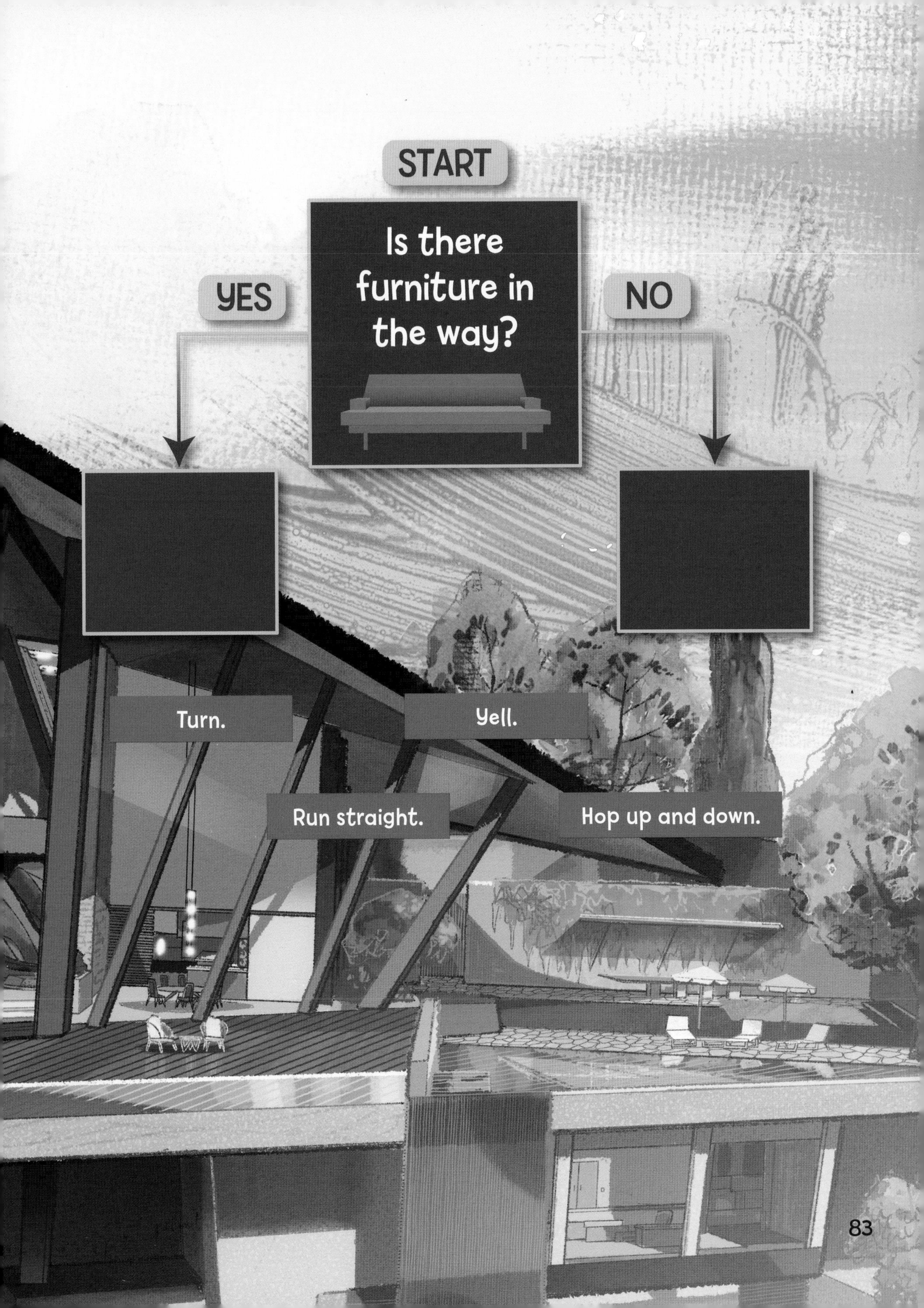

START

Is there furniture in the way?

YES

NO

Turn.

Yell.

Run straight.

Hop up and down.

The house has lots of rooms! Dash wants to explore all of them. He looks behind each door he finds. If he's already seen a room, he keeps moving. But if it's a new room, he explores! On your own paper, draw a blank flowchart like the one on the next page. Use the list of labels to fill in the flowchart. When you're finished, make sure the flowchart helps Dash explore new rooms.

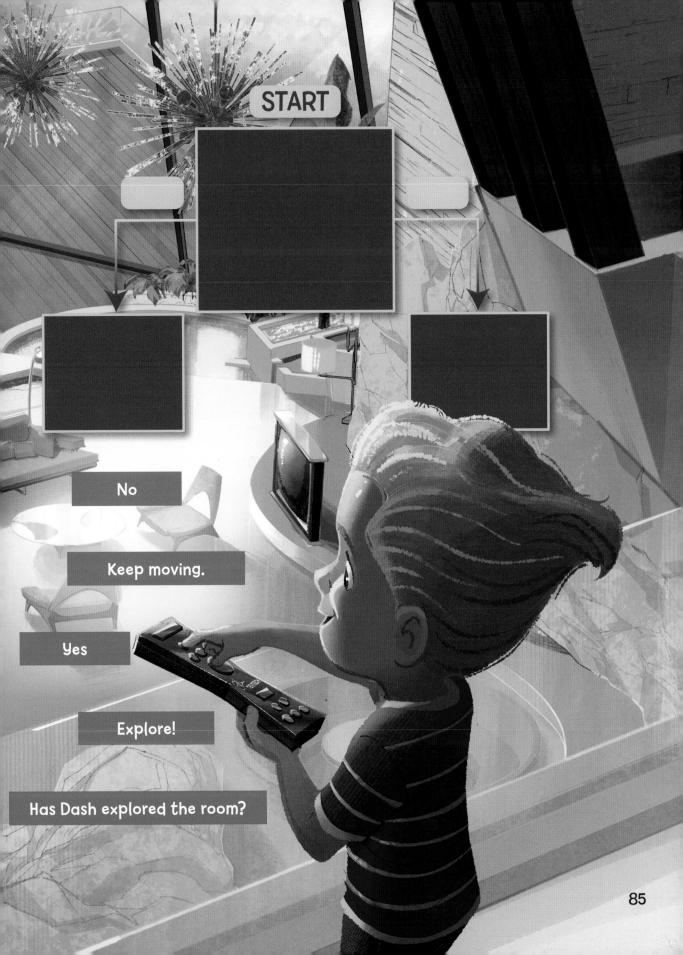

START

No

Keep moving.

Yes

Explore!

Has Dash explored the room?

Elastigirl on a Mission, Part 1

The MetroLev train is out of control! Elastigirl chases it across the city's rooftops on her Elasticycle.

Some lines of code have bugs, or errors. That means the code won't work properly. Each time Elastigirl comes to a gap between buildings, she must jump to the next roof. Look at the three flowcharts on page 87. Two of the flowcharts have bugs. Choose the flowchart with no bugs that will help Elastigirl catch the MetroLev.

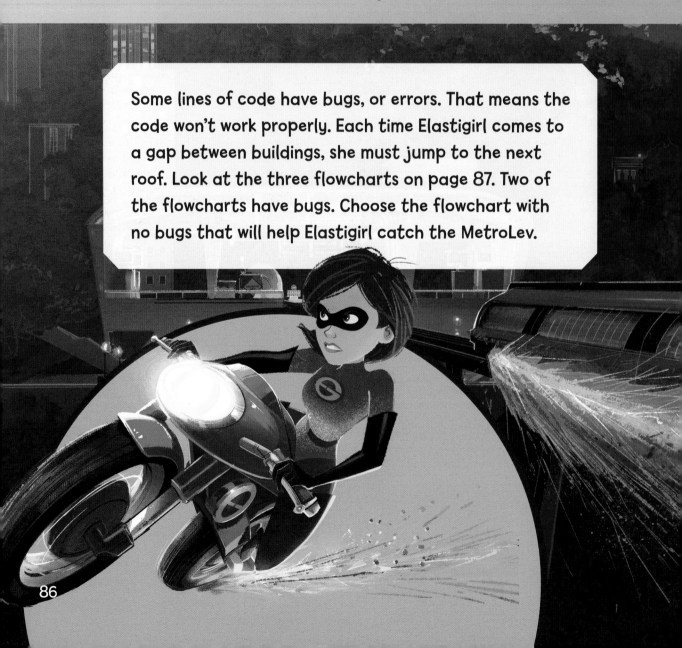

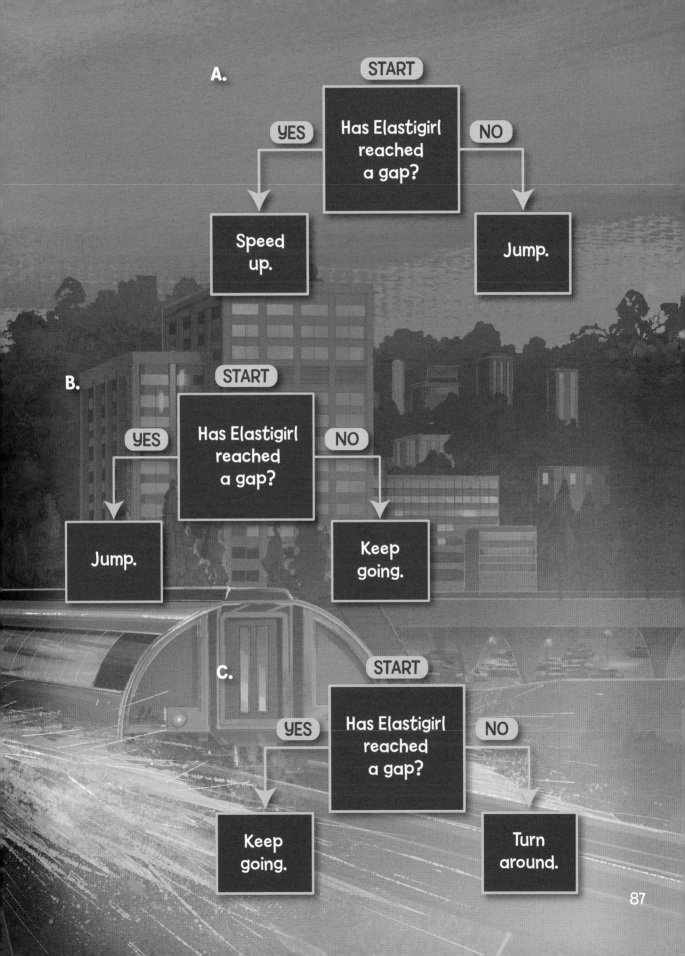

Bob's in Charge

Bob is watching the kids on his own. It's Jack-Jack's bedtime. Everything's going fine until Jack-Jack shoots laser beams from his eyes!

Sometimes code has more than one condition. Bob needs to catch Jack-Jack before he can put him to bed. Jack-Jack also needs to stop using his powers. The flowchart on the next page has a blank space where the second condition should go. Choose the answer that will let Bob put Jack-Jack to bed.

A. Did Jack-Jack finish his dinner?

B. Is Jack-Jack in bed?

C. Is Jack-Jack using his powers?

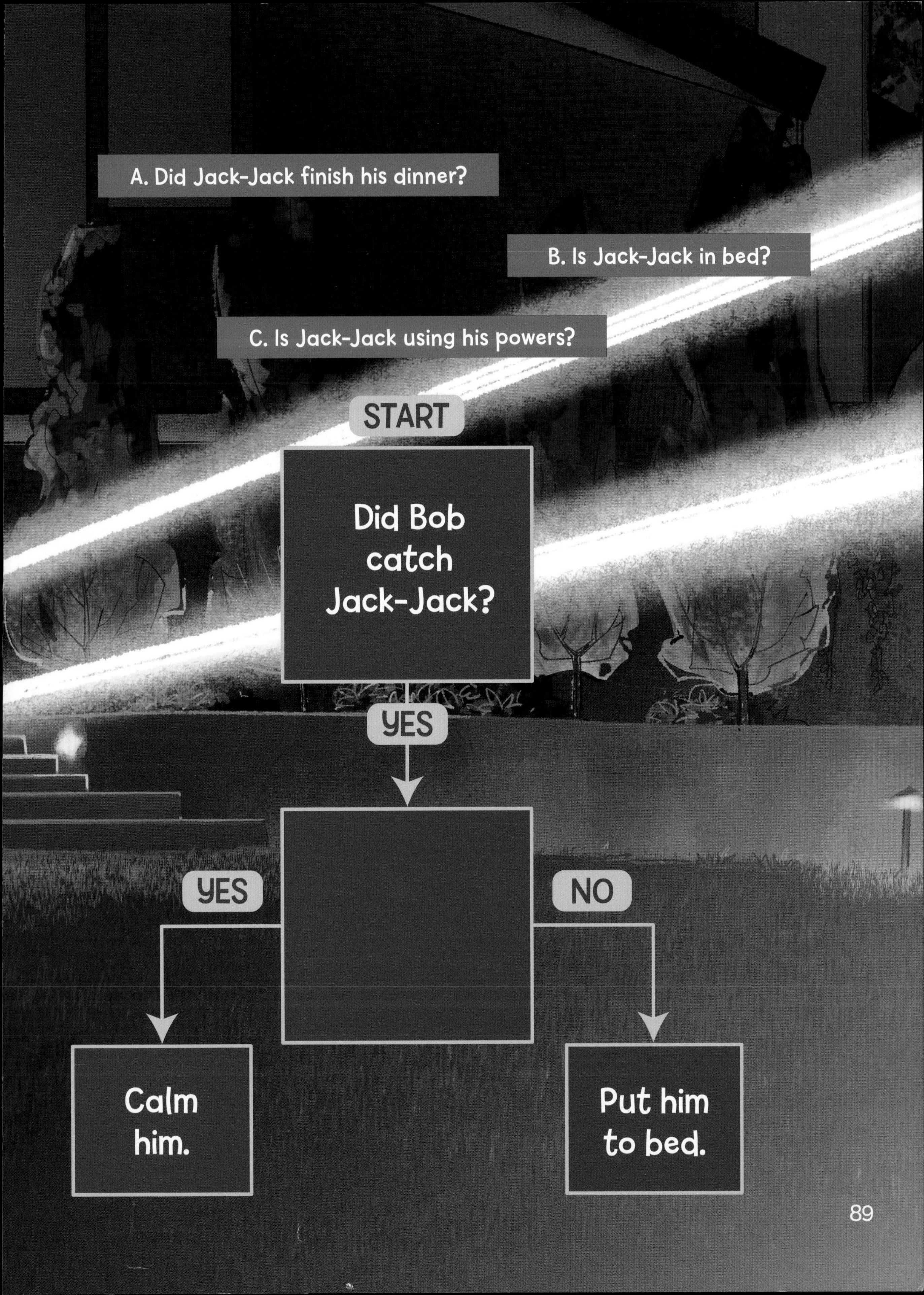

START

Did Bob catch Jack-Jack?

YES

YES

NO

Calm him.

Put him to bed.

Elastigirl on a Mission, Part 2

The Screenslaver is attacking a helicopter! Elastigirl needs to rescue the woman on board. But first, she has to find her.

Get a partner and a small stuffed animal. Pretend the stuffed animal is the woman in danger. You are Elastigirl. Close your eyes, and ask your partner to hide the woman somewhere in the room. Don't peek! When your partner is finished, open your eyes. Follow the flowchart on page 91 to find the woman. You can save her by picking her up. When you're finished, switch and have your partner search.

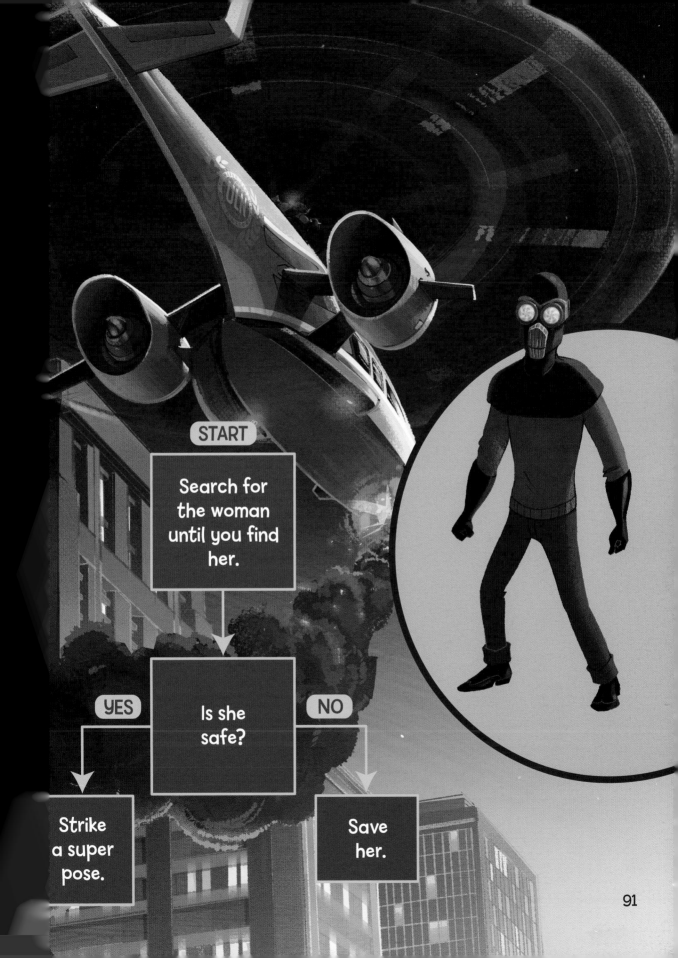

START

Search for the woman until you find her.

YES   Is she safe?   NO

Strike a super pose.

Save her.

91

Supers Attack!

Supers under Screenslaver's control attack Jack-Jack, Dash, and Violet at home. They need to find a way to escape, fast!

When you brush your teeth, you move the brush in circles. You repeat the same step until your teeth are clean. Sometimes code must repeat steps too. Code with a loop repeats until a condition is met.

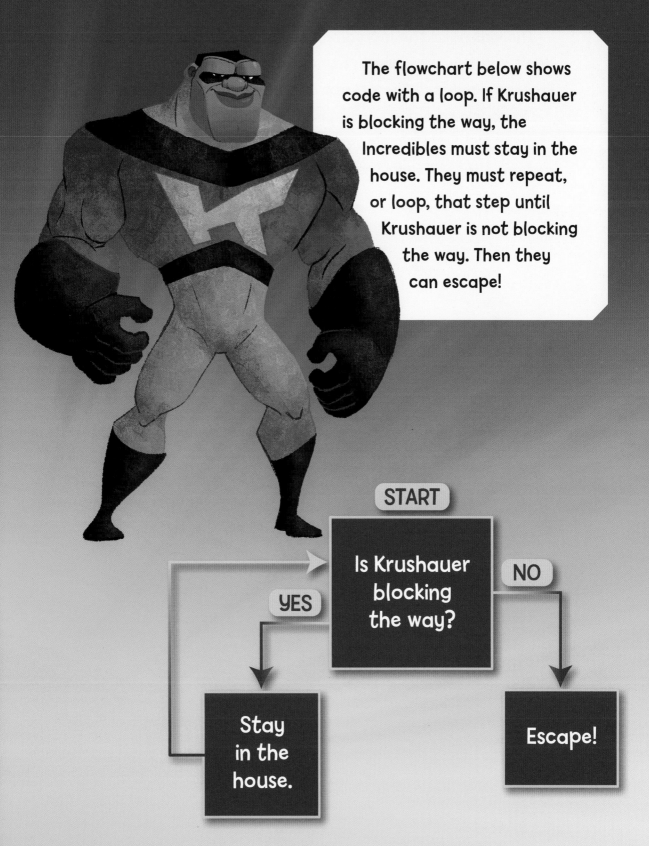

The flowchart below shows code with a loop. If Krushauer is blocking the way, the Incredibles must stay in the house. They must repeat, or loop, that step until Krushauer is not blocking the way. Then they can escape!

START

Is Krushauer blocking the way?

YES

NO

Stay in the house.

Escape!

The kids need the Incredibile to get away. But they can't call the car if they're under attack. Maybe Frozone can block the attack and buy them some time.

On your own paper, draw the flowchart on this page. Look at the list of actions. Fill in your flowchart with actions that will help the Incredibles escape.

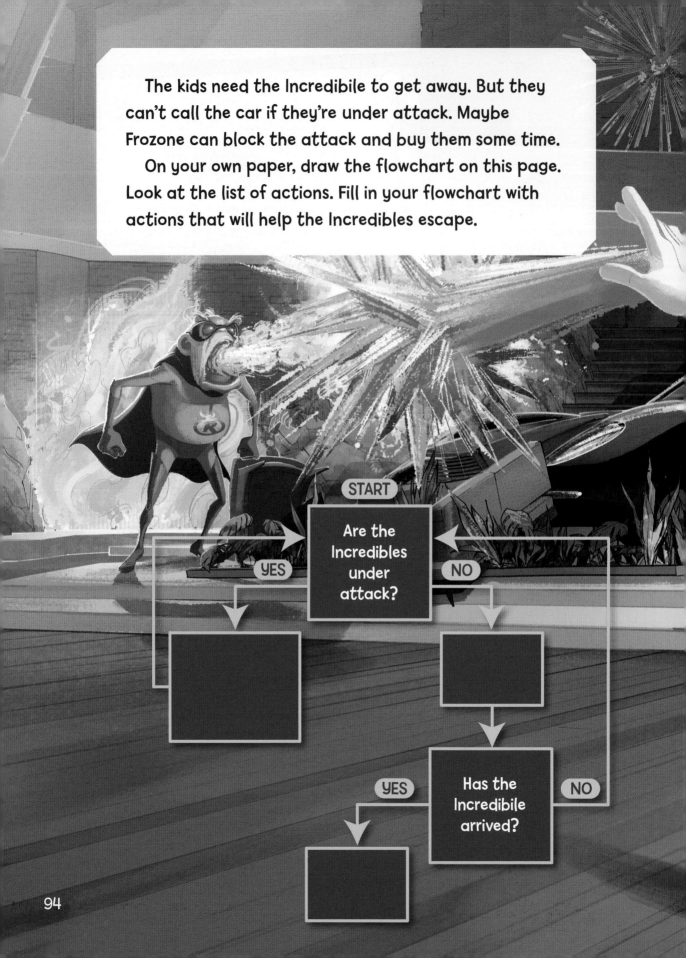

START

Are the Incredibles under attack?

YES

NO

Has the Incredibile arrived?

YES

NO

Drive away!

Frozone blocks the attack!

Call the Incredibile.

95

Mr. Incredible and Elastigirl Need Help

Violet, Dash, and Jack-Jack are racing to the DevTech boat in the Incredibile. Their parents are in trouble!

The Incredibile is an amazing machine. It can zoom down the road as a superfast car. On the water, it can turn into a boat! Look at the flowchart on the next page, and find the bugs, or places where the code won't work. Remember that when the Incredibile is on land, it needs to be a car. It should be a boat on the water. How would you rewrite the flowchart to fix the bugs?

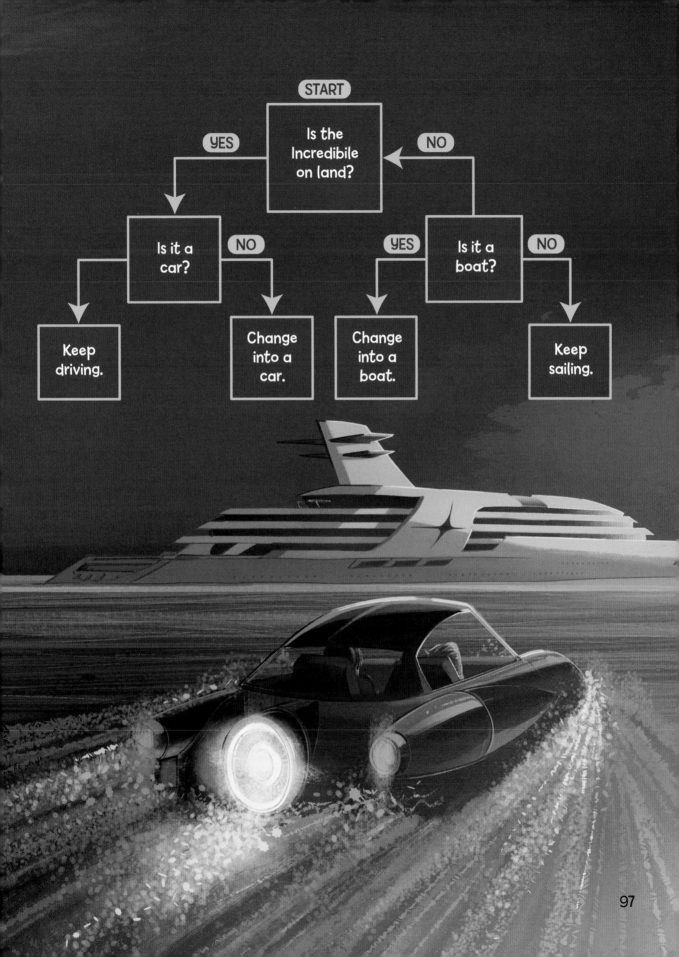

START

Is the Incredibile on land?

YES

NO

Is it a car?

NO

Is it a boat?

YES

NO

Keep driving.

Change into a car.

Change into a boat.

Keep sailing.

Battle!

The kids found their parents on the DevTech boat. They need to fight together to defeat Supers under the Screenslaver's power.

Grab a pair of dice and at least one person to play this game with you. Decide who will be the Incredibles and who will be other Supers. Then look at the conditional flowchart on the next page for the rules. To start, each player rolls one of the dice. Follow the conditions and loops in the flowchart to play the game. Who will get ten points first? The winner of the game wins the battle!

START

Both players roll.

YES — Did you roll the same number? — NO

The player with the higher number scores a point.

YES — Do all players have fewer than ten points? — NO

The player with ten points wins!

If you don't have dice, you can make stacks of six cards with the numbers 1-6 on them.

After you play a few times, make up your own rules. On your own paper, create a new flowchart that shows how the new rules work. One new rule might be that only odd numbers count. Another might be that the lowest roll wins. Or maybe rolling a certain number makes you win instantly!

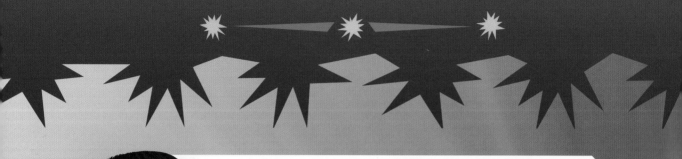

You've learned so much about conditionals that you might start seeing them everywhere. If you think about it, lots of times conditionals help you make decisions. Do you have something to say at school? If the answer is yes, you might raise your hand. Is it raining during recess? Then maybe you will play in the gym instead.

Think about conditionals when you're at home too.
Is your room clean? If so, you can go outside and play.
But if it isn't, you might have to stay in and clean your
room. Do you need help with your homework? If you do,
ask someone. If not, take care of it yourself. You might be
surprised by how often conditionals come up in your life!

Answer Key

Algorithms with *Frozen*

Page 8–9: 1. A; 2. B; 3. C

Page 11 (possible answers):

⬇➡➡⬇⬇⬇➡➡ or ⬇⬇⬇➡➡⬇➡➡

Pages 14–15: wall 1 = A; ceiling = B; wall 2 = C

Page 17 (possible answer):

⬇➡ 3(⬆) 3(➡) 2(⬆) 5(⬅)

Page 27:

Answer Key
Looping with *Finding Dory*

Page 33: A

Page 34: A

Page 35: B

Page 37: 3(➡️) 3(⬆️) Bark! (*possible answer*)

Page 41: ➡️⬇️6(➡️) 2(⬇️) (*possible answer*)

Page 47: 3(2⬇️, 3 ➡️)

Page 49: 3(➡️) listen 3(⬆️) listen 4(➡️) listen 3(⬇️) listen 3(➡️) listen 2(➡️)

Bugs and Errors with *Wreck-It Ralph*

Page 55: B

Page 57: ⬆➡➡➡➡➡➡

Page 61: ⬆⬆⬆⬆⬅⬅⬅⬆⬆➡

Page 69: ➡〰➡〰

➡〰➡〰〰➡

〰➡〰〰〰➡〰➡

Page 73: 2(⬆) 2(push) 2(➡) 2(⬆) 3(push) ➡ 3(⬆)

Answer Key

Conditionals with *Incredibles 2*

Page 81: B

Page 83:

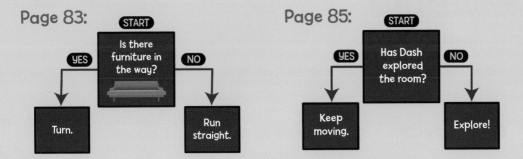

START
Is there furniture in the way?

YES → Turn.

NO → Run straight.

Page 85:

START
Has Dash explored the room?

YES → Keep moving.

NO → Explore!

Page 87: B

Page 89: C

Pages 94-95:

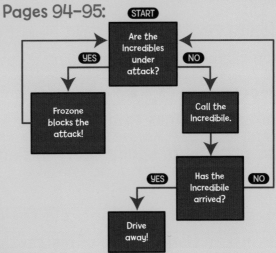

START
Are the Incredibles under attack?

YES → Frozone blocks the attack!

NO → Call the Incredibile.

Has the Incredibile arrived?

YES → Drive away!

NO

Page 97:

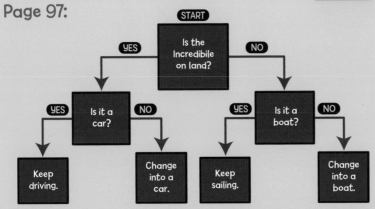

START
Is the Incredibile on land?

YES → Is it a car?

YES → Keep driving.

NO → Change into a car.

NO → Is it a boat?

YES → Keep sailing.

NO → Change into a boat.

Glossary

algorithm: a group of instructions, made up of lines of code, that tells your computer how to solve a problem or finish a job

bug: a mistake found in lines of code

code: instructions for computers that are written in a way that computers can follow

condition: something that must happen before something else happens

decompose: to take a big problem and break it down into small pieces to figure it out

do-until loop: a loop that continues until a condition is met

loop: a line of code that tells the computer to repeat an instruction or a set of instructions a certain number of times

resolve: to fix a mistake (a bug) in lines of code

run: to start a program

Further Information

CodeMonkey
https://www.playcodemonkey.com

Code.org
https://code.org/learn

Kelly, James F. *The Story of Coding*. New York: DK, 2017.

Lyons, Heather. *Coding in the Real World*. Minneapolis: Lerner Publications, 2018.

Lyons, Heather, and Elizabeth Tweedale. *Coding, Bugs, and Fixes*. Minneapolis: Lerner Publications, 2017.

Lyons, Heather, and Elizabeth Tweedale. *Learn to Program*. Minneapolis: Lerner Publications, 2017.

Matteson, Adrienne. *Coding with Scratch Jr.* Ann Arbor, MI: Cherry Lake, 2017.

Prottsman, Kiki. *My First Coding Book*. New York: DK, 2017.

Index

About the Author

Allyssa Loya is an elementary school librarian in North Texas. Her passion for bringing meaningful learning to students led her to cultivate a technology-forward library that includes a makerspace and a coding club. While running the coding club in the library, she realized how important it is for every student to experience coding. Not every student will grow up to be a computer programmer, but all students will need to know how to think clearly and critically when they are adults.

Loya is married to an IT manager, who is a perfect support system for her technological endeavors. Her two young boys are a constant reminder of the experiences that all students deserve from their educators.

Lerner Publications Company
A division of Lerner Publishing Group, Inc.
241 First Avenue North
Minneapolis, MN 55401 USA

For reading levels and more information, look up this title at www.lernerbooks.com.

Additional graphics provided by Laura Westlund/Independent Picture Service.

Main body text set in Billy Infant Regular 14/20.
Typeface provided by SparkyType.

Library of Congress Cataloging-in-Publication Data
The Cataloging-in-Publication Data for *Disney Coding Adventures: First Steps for Kid
    Coders* is on file at the Library of Congress.
ISBN 978-1-5415-4249-5 (pbk.)
ISBN 978-1-5415-4252-5 (eb pdf)

Manufactured in the United States of America
1-45414-39603-5/10/2018